answers to
WHAT WOULD JESUS DO?

by Beverly Courrege

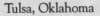

HONOR
BOOKS

Tulsa, Oklahoma

answers to What Would Jesus Do?
ISBN 1-56292-462-1
Copyright © 1997 Beverly Courrege
9230 Markville
Dallas, Texas 75243

4th Printing

Published by **Honor Books, Inc.**
P.O. Box 55388
Tulsa, OK 74155

Introduction

WWJD. You've seen it everywhere lately — on bracelets, dog tags, key chains, T-shirts, hats, even backpacks! But what does it mean? WWJD is an acronym for "What Would Jesus Do?"

Every day we have a choice: To do things God's way or the world's way. Jesus is our example to follow, and He only did those things He saw God the Father doing. (See John 5:19.) This book, *Answers to: What Would Jesus Do?*, provides simple reminders of how Jesus lived his life on earth.

So keep this book handy — in your coat pocket, your desk drawer, or your school locker — and you will have a ready answer for any situation you may face!

What Would Jesus Do?

W W
J D

HE WOULD USE HIS GIFTS

God has given us special talents and abilities to use for Him.

4

**The Creator has not given you
a longing to do that which
you have no ability to do.**

Now God gives us many kinds of special
abilities, but it is the same Holy Spirit who is
the source of them all. The Holy Spirit
displays God's power through each of us as
a means of helping the entire church. It is
the same and only Holy Spirit who gives all
these gifts and powers, deciding which each
one of us should have.

I Corinthians 12:4,7,11 TLB

5

What

Would

Jesus

Do?

W W
J D

HE WOULD THANK GOD ALWAYS

When we pray, we should always thank God for what He has done and for everything He will do.

Some people think God does not like to be troubled with our constant coming and asking. The only way to trouble God is not to come at all.

Do not be anxious about anything, but in everything, by prayer and petition, with thanksgiving, present your requests to God.

Philippians 4:6

What

Would

Jesus

Do?

W W
J D

HE WOULD STORE TREASURES IN HEAVEN

Jesus told us nothing destroys true treasures — those things that are important to God.

Aim at heaven, and you will get earth thrown in; aim at earth, and you will get neither.

"Do not store up for yourselves treasures on earth, where moth and rust destroy, and where thieves break in and steal. But store up for yourselves treasures in heaven, where moth and rust do not destroy, and where thieves do not break in and steal. For where your treasure is, there your heart will be also."

Matthew 6:19-21

What

Would

Jesus

Do?

W W
J D

HE WOULD TREAT OTHERS THE WAY HE WANTED TO BE TREATED

You cannot expect others to be nice to you if you are not nice to them.

We have committed the Golden Rule to memory.

Let us now commit it to life.

"So in everything, do to others what you would have them do to you, for this sums up the Law and the Prophets."

Matthew 7:12

What

Would

Jesus

Do?

W W
J D

HE WOULD GIVE
CHEERFULLY

God is always pleased with us when we are happy to give.

Money, *n.* **A blessing that is of no advantage to us excepting when we part with it.**

I want each of you to take plenty of time to think it over, and make up your own mind what you will give. That will protect you against sob stories and arm-twisting. God loves it when the giver delights in the giving.

2 Corinthians 9:7 THE MESSAGE

What

Would

Jesus

Do?

W W
J D

HE WOULD BEHAVE
PROPERLY

*It is important that our actions reflect
God in our lives.*

Example is not the main thing in influencing others.

It is the only thing.

Be decent and true in everything you do so that all can approve your behavior. Don't spend your time in wild parties and getting drunk or in adultery and lust, or fighting, or jealousy. But ask the Lord Jesus Christ to help you live as you should, and don't make plans to enjoy evil.

Romans 13:13-14 TLB

W | W
J | D

What
Would
Jesus
Do?

HE WOULD ALWAYS FORGIVE

Jesus told us God cannot forgive our sins if we do not forgive others.

16

A wise man will make haste to forgive, because he knows the true value of time, and will not suffer it to pass away in unnecessary pain.

"For if you forgive men when they sin against you, your heavenly Father will also forgive you. But if you do not forgive men their sins, your Father will not forgive your sins."

Matthew 6:14-15

answers to

What
Would
Jesus
Do?

W | W
J | D

HE WOULD YIELD TO GOD

God will help us do what He wants us to do, we just have to let Him!

18

Give me a task too big, too hard for human hands, then I shall come at length to lean on thee, and leaning find my strength.

God is working in you to help you want to do and be able to do what pleases him.

Philippians 2:13 NCV

answers to

What Would Jesus Do?

W W
J D

HE WOULD PLEASE GOD

Jesus only did what was pleasing to God.

The true guide of our conduct is no outward authority, but the voice of God, who comes down to dwell in our souls, who knows all our thoughts.

So Jesus said, "When you have killed the Messiah, then you will realize that I am he and that I have not been telling you my own ideas, but have spoken what the Father taught me. And he who sent me is with me — he has not deserted me — for I always do those things that are pleasing to him."

John 8:28-29 TLB

answers to

What Would Jesus Do?

W W
J D

HE WOULD CHOOSE HIS FRIENDS WISELY

Jesus prayed all night before choosing the twelve disciples who would be His closest friends.

Let your friends be the friends of your deliberate choice.

One of those days Jesus went out to a mountainside to pray, and spent the night praying to God.

Luke 6:12

W W
J D

What
Would
Jesus
Do?

HE WOULD HAVE THE RIGHT MOTIVES

Jesus would do His work for God, rather than for praise from people.

It is far more impressive when others discover your good qualities without your help.

"Be careful! When you do good things, don't do them in front of people to be seen by them. If you do that, you will have no reward from your Father in heaven."

Matthew 6:1 NCV

W W
J D

What

Would

Jesus

Do?

HE WOULD
LOVE HIS
ENEMIES

*Jesus told us to love our enemies and
to pray for them.*

Those who deserve love the least need it the most.

"But I tell you: Love your enemies and pray for those who persecute you, that you may be sons of your Father in heaven. He causes his sun to rise on the evil and the good, and sends rain on the righteous and the unrighteous."

Matthew 5:44-45

What Would Jesus Do?

W W
J D

HE WOULD LOVE HIS NEIGHBOR

Really loving your neighbor means never sinning against them by disobeying any of God's commandments.

Love is love's reward.

The law code — don't sleep with another person's spouse, don't take someone's life, don't take what isn't yours, don't always be wanting what you don't have, and any other "don't" you can think of — finally adds up to this: Love other people as well as you do yourself. You can't go wrong when you love others. When you add up everything in the law code, the sum total is love.

Romans 13:9-11 THE MESSAGE

W W
J D

What Would Jesus Do?

HE WOULD OBEY HIS PARENTS

God promises us prosperity and long life when we honor our parents by obeying them.

Obedience is the "virtue-making virtue."

Children, obey your parents as the Lord wants, because this is the right thing to do. The command says, "Honor your father and mother." This is the first command that has a promise with it — "Then everything will be well with you, and you will have a long life on the earth."

Ephesians 6:1-3 NCV

What

Would

Jesus

Do?

W | W
J | D

HE WOULD DRAW NEAR TO GOD

Jesus walked in the presence of God at all times.

Prayer is a rising up and drawing near to God in mind, and in heart, and in spirit.

Come near to God and he will come near to you. Wash your hands, you sinners, and purify your hearts, you double-minded. Humble yourselves before the Lord, and he will lift you up.

James 4:8,10

W | W
J | D

What

Would

Jesus

Do?

HE WOULD PRAY FOR OTHER BELIEVERS

Jesus prayed for His friends who were doing God's work.

The best way to remember people is in prayer.

"My plea is not for the world but for those you have given me because they belong to you. Now I am leaving the world, and leaving them behind, and coming to you. Holy Father, keep them in your own care — all those you have given me — so that they will be united just as we are, with none missing. I'm not asking you to take them out of the world, but to keep them safe from Satan's power."

John 17:9,11,15 TLB

35

answers to

What
Would
Jesus
Do?

W | W
J | D

**HE WOULD
TRUST GOD
COMPLETELY**

*Jesus trusted God to raise Lazarus
from the dead.*

The prayer that begins with trustfulness, and passes on into waiting, will always end in thankfulness, triumph, and praise.

...Jesus looked up and said, "Father, I thank you that you have heard me. I knew that you always hear me, but I said this for the benefit of the people standing here, that they may believe that you sent me." When he had said this, Jesus called in a loud voice, "Lazarus, come out!" The dead man came out, his hands and feet wrapped with strips of linen, and a cloth around his face.

John 11:41-44

37

answers to

What

Would

Jesus

Do?

W	W
J	D

HE WOULD KEEP HIS PRIORITIES STRAIGHT

We should seek first the kingdom of God, because when we do, everything else falls into place.

Success is...seeking, knowing, loving, and obeying God. If you seek, you will know; if you know, you will love; if you love, you will obey.

"But seek first his kingdom and his righteousness, and all these things will be given to you as well."

Matthew 6:33

W W
J D

What

Would

Jesus

Do?

HE WOULD BE AN EXAMPLE

We have been called to follow the example of Jesus' life and, in turn, be an example to others.

**Keep company with good men
and good men you will
imitate.**

This suffering is all part of the work God has
given you. Christ, who suffered for you, is
your example. Follow in his steps.

I Peter 2:21 TLB

answers to

What

Would

Jesus

Do?

W	W
J	D

**HE WOULD VALUE
ALL LIFE**

Everything and everyone is God's creation.

All of creation is a song of praise to God.

"The God who made the world and everything in it...Starting from scratch, he made the entire human race and made the earth hospitable, with plenty of time and space for living so we could seek after God, and not just grope around in the dark but actually find him."

Acts 17:24-27 THE MESSAGE

43

answers to

What

Would

Jesus

Do?

W W
J D

HE WOULD WALK IN TRUTH

When we walk in the truth we are walking in a manner worthy of God.

Keep true, never be ashamed of doing right; decide on what you know is right and stick to it.

Some of the brothers traveling by have made me very happy by telling me that your life stays clean and true, and that you are living by the standards of the Gospel. I could have no greater joy than to hear such things about my children.

3 John 3-4 TLB

answers to

What
Would
Jesus
Do?

W W
J D

HE WOULD PRAY ALL THE TIME

Jesus was ready to pray each moment of the day or night.

Prayer should be the key of the morning and the lock of the night.

Pray all the time.

I Thessalonians 5:17 THE MESSAGE

answers to

What

Would

Jesus

Do?

W W
J D

HE WOULD STAND FIRM

We must stand firm in truth, righteousness, and peace.

In trying times, don't quit trying.

Stand firm then, with the belt of truth buckled around your waist, with the breastplate of righteousness in place, and with your feet fitted with the readiness that comes from the gospel of peace.

Ephesians 6:14-15

answers to

What
Would
Jesus
Do?

W	W
J	D

HE WOULD KNOW
SCRIPTURE

We cannot give others the Word of God if
we do not know the Scripture!

50

The best law for Bible study is the law of perseverance. The psalmist says, "I have stuck unto thy testimonies...." Some people are like express trains; they skim along so quickly that they see nothing.

Then he started at the beginning, with the Books of Moses, and went on through all the Prophets, pointing out everything in the Scriptures that referred to him.

Luke 24:27 THE MESSAGE

What
Would
Jesus
Do?

HE WOULD BOAST ONLY ABOUT GOD

Jesus was boastful about the works of God, never about himself.

The greatest act of faith is when man decides he is not God.

But, "Let him who boasts boast in the Lord." For it is not the one who commends himself who is approved, but the one whom the Lord commends.

2 Corinthians 10:17-18

W W
J D

What

Would

Jesus

Do?

HE WOULD AVOID PRIDEFUL WORDS

Jesus warns us not to use words of pride to make ourselves look good to other people.

Pride: the first peer and president of hell.

"The Pharisee stood alone and prayed, 'God, I thank you that I am not like other people who steal, cheat, or take part in adultery.' The tax collector, standing at a distance, would not even look up to heaven. But he beat on his chest because he was so sad. He said, 'God, have mercy on me, a sinner.' ...All who make themselves great will be made humble, but all who make themselves humble will be made great."

Luke 18:11,13-14 NCV

W W
J D

What
Would
Jesus
Do?

HE WOULD
OVERLOOK AN
INSULT

Jesus endured the insults of the soldiers as they stripped His clothes from Him, put a crown of thorns on His head, spit in His face, and used a staff to beat Him.

In taking revenge, a man is but even with his enemy; but in passing it over, he is superior.

They stripped him and put a scarlet robe on him, and then twisted together a crown of thorns and set it on his head. They put a staff in his right hand and knelt in front of him and mocked him. "Hail, king of the Jews!" they said. They spit on him, and took the staff and struck him on the head again and again.

Matthew 27:28-30

What

Would

Jesus

Do?

W | W
J | D

HE WOULD HAVE COMPASSION FOR SINNERS

Jesus told those who have been saved to have compassion for those who are lost.

Kindness has converted more people than zeal, science, or eloquence.

When he saw the crowds, he had compassion on them, because they were harassed and helpless, like sheep without a shepherd.

Matthew 9:36 NIV

What

Would

Jesus

Do?

W	W
J	D

HE WOULD FORGIVE EVEN THE WORST POSSIBLE HURT

When Jesus was hanging on the cross he cried out to God to forgive those who were responsible.

We pardon in the degree that we love.

Jesus said, "Father, forgive them, because they don't know what they are doing."

Luke 23:34 NCV

W W
J D

What

Would

Jesus

Do?

HE WOULD HAVE THE HEART OF GOD

Jesus was loving, kind, gentle, forgiving, and peaceful and He wants us to be the same.

It's good to be a Christian and know it, but it's better to be a Christian and show it!

Therefore, as God's chosen people, holy and dearly loved, clothe yourselves with compassion, kindness, humility, gentleness and patience. Bear with each other and forgive whatever grievances you may have against one another. Forgive as the Lord forgave you. And whatever you do, whether in word or deed, do it all in the name of the Lord Jesus....

Colossians 3:12-13,17

What Would Jesus Do?

W | W
J | D

HE WOULD BE OPTIMISTIC

Jesus wants us to see beyond temporary setbacks and focus on the promise of the future.

Few cases of eyestrain have been developed by looking on the bright side of things.

I know how to live on almost nothing or with everything. I have learned the secret of contentment in every situation, whether it be a full stomach or hunger, plenty or want; for I can do everything God asks me to with the help of Christ who gives me the strength and power.

Philippians 4:12-13 TLB

What

Would

Jesus

Do?

W	W
J	D

HE WOULD SHOW APPRECIATION

Jesus wants us to show appreciation to those who help us grow up in the Lord.

Do not save your loving speeches
For your friends till they are dead;
Do not write them on their
tombstones,
Speak them rather now instead.

Welcome him in the Lord with great joy, and show your appreciation.

Philippians 2:29 TLB

answers to

What

Would

Jesus

Do?

W | W
—————
J | D

HE WOULD HAVE COURAGE TO REACH OUT TO THOSE WHO HURT HIM

When Jesus was dying on the cross, He asked God to forgive those who had put Him there.

68

Never does the human soul appear so strong as when it forgoes revenge and dares to forgive an injury.

Jesus said, "Father, forgive them, because they don't know what they are doing."

Luke 23:34 NCV

What

Would

Jesus

Do?

W W
J D

HE WOULD ENCOUNTER TRIALS WITH JOY

We should be happy to face trials because they help make us more like Jesus.

Happiness is the result of circumstances, but joy endures in spite of circumstances.

Consider it pure joy, my brothers, whenever you face trials of many kinds, because you know that the testing of your faith develops perseverance.

James 1:2-3

W W
J D

What

Would

Jesus

Do?

HE WOULD KNOW SERVING OTHERS IS SERVING GOD

Serving others demonstrates the love, joy, and peace we have received from God.

One thing I know: the ones among you who will be really happy are those who have sought and found how to serve.

In all the work you are doing, work the best you can. Work as if you were doing it for the Lord, not for people. Remember that you will receive your reward from the Lord, which he promised to his people. You are serving the Lord Christ.

Colossians 3:23-24 NCV

W W
J D

What

Would

Jesus

Do?

HE WOULD HELP OTHERS RETURN TO GOD WHEN THEY STRAY FROM HIM

When someone wanders off from God we must help them turn back to Him.

74

A true friend never gets in your way unless you happen to be going down.

Dear brothers, if anyone has slipped away from God and no longer trusts the Lord and someone helps him understand the Truth again, that person who brings him back to God will have saved a wandering soul from death, bringing about the forgiveness of his many sins.

James 5:19-20 TLB

HE WOULD ACCEPT ALL PEOPLE

Jesus died for everyone. He wants us to accept all people — red, yellow, black, or white.

Every human being is intended to have a character of his own — to be what no other is, and to do what no other can do.

So, warmly welcome each other into the church, just as Christ has warmly welcomed you; then God will be glorified. Remember that Jesus Christ came to show that God is true to his promises and to help the Jews. And remember that he came also that the Gentiles might be saved and give glory to God for his mercies to them.

Romans 15:7-9 TLB

77

What

Would

Jesus

Do?

W W
J D

HE WOULD PAY A DEBT

We should always repay our debts, but we never stop owing the debt of love.

The love we give away is the only love we keep.

Let no debt remain outstanding, except the continuing debt to love one another, for he who loves his fellowman has fulfilled the law.

Romans 13:8

answers to

What

Would

Jesus

Do?

W W
J D

**HE WOULD GO TO
CHURCH**

*Each of us are a necessary member of our
church and when we are not there
we are missed.*

Church attendance is as vital to a disciple as a transfusion of rich, healthy blood to a sick man.

If each part of the body were the same part, there would be no body. But truly God put the parts, each one of them, in the body as he wanted them. So then there are many parts, but only one body.

I Corinthians 12:18-20 NCV

W W
J D

What Would Jesus Do?

HE WOULD COMPETE WITH FAIRNESS

When we compete at anything we must exercise self-control so we are not disqualified from the competition.

Obstacles are those frightful things you see when you take your eyes off the goal.

To win the contest you must deny yourselves many things that would keep you from doing your best. An athlete goes to all this trouble just to win a blue ribbon or a silver cup, but we do it for a heavenly reward that never disappears. So I run straight to the goal with purpose in every step. I fight to win. I'm not just shadow boxing or playing around.

I Corinthians 9:25-26 TLB

W W
J D

What

Would

Jesus

Do?

HE WOULD TELL A FRIEND RIGHT FROM WRONG IN A LOVING WAY

If we see a friend sinning we must go to him and correct him from a pure heart, a clear conscience, and a sincere faith that is motivated by love!

To have a good friend is one of the highest delights of life; to be a good friend is one of the noblest and most difficult undertakings.

The goal of this command is love, which comes from a pure heart and a good conscience and a sincere faith.

I Timothy 1:5

answers to

What

Would

Jesus

Do?

W   W
J   D

HE WOULD ENCOURAGE A FRIEND THROUGH A DISAPPOINTMENT

Although we may face disappointments in spite of the effort we put forth, God never forgets any of our work.

We should seize every opportunity to give encouragement. Encouragement is oxygen to the soul.

God is not unjust; he will not forget your work and the love you have shown him as you have helped his people and continue to help them.

Hebrews 6:10

W W
J D

What

Would

Jesus

Do?

HE WOULD GIVE THE COAT OFF HIS BACK

Jesus told us to give anyone anything they ask from us.

It is better to give than to lend, and it costs about the same.

Give to those who ask, and don't turn away from those who want to borrow.

Matthew 5:42 TLB

W W
J D

What

Would

Jesus

Do?

HE WOULD TURN THE OTHER CHEEK

Jesus told us there would be times when we must accept the wrongs done against us.

Patience serves as a protection against wrongs as clothes do against cold. For if you put on more clothes as the cold increases, it will have no power to hurt you. So in like manner, you must grow in patience when you meet with great wrongs, and they will be powerless to vex you.

"But I tell you, Do not resist an evil person. If someone strikes you on the right cheek, turn to him the other also."

Matthew 5:39

W | W
J | D

What

Would

Jesus

Do?

**HE WOULD
HELP THE
HOMELESS**

*Jesus told us we must treat the poor,
crippled, and lame — anyone who cannot
repay us — exactly the way we would
treat our favorite friends.*

Goodness is love in action, love with its hand to the plow, love with the burden on its back, love following His footsteps who went about continually doing good.

"Instead, invite the poor, the crippled, the lame, and the blind. Then at the resurrection of the godly, God will reward you for inviting those who can't repay you."

Luke 14:13-14 TLB

answers to

What Would Jesus Do?

W W
J D

HE WOULD OBEY THE RULES

Rules that come from the governing authorities we live under are made for our good to help prevent bad things other people may want to do.

He that has learned to obey will know how to command.

Obey the government for God is the one who has put it there. There is no government anywhere that God has not placed in power. So those who refuse to obey the laws of the land are refusing to obey God, and punishment will follow.

Romans 13:1-2 TLB

answers to

What

Would

Jesus

Do?

W   W

J   D

HE WOULD AVOID EMPTY CHATTER

Any discussions that are not encouraging and wholesome may lead us into sinful words.

Blessed is the man who, having nothing to say, abstains from giving in words evidence of the fact.

Stay away from foolish, useless talk, because that will lead people further away from God. Their evil teaching will spread like a sickness inside the body.

2 Timothy 2:16-17 NCV

What
Would
Jesus
Do?

W | W
J | D

HE WOULD AVOID TROUBLEMAKERS

The Bible warns us that there are many proud, disobedient, ungrateful, bad people that will want to make our life as a Christian difficult. Try to avoid them!

Keep away from people who try to belittle your ambitions. Small people always do that, but the really great people make you feel that you, too, can become great.

In the last days there will be many troubles, because people will love themselves, love money, brag, and be proud. They will say evil things against others and will not obey their parents or be thankful or be the kind of people God wants. They will...act as if they serve God but will not have his power. Stay away from those people.

2 Timothy 3:1-2,5 NCV

answers to

What

Would

Jesus

Do?

W W
J D

HE WOULD MAKE THE RIGHT CHOICES

Jesus would always choose obedience to God over the ungodliness of sinful choices.

Conformity is the jailer of freedom and the enemy of growth.

If he rescued Lot, a righteous man, who was distressed by the filthy lives of lawless men...then the Lord knows how to rescue godly men from trials and to hold the unrighteous for the day of judgment.

2 Peter 2:7,9

What Would Jesus Do?

W W
J D

HE WOULD BE ALERT TO SIN

Jesus suffered for us so we would not have to stay in the company of evil friends who want us to be like them.

I make it a rule of Christian duty never to go to a place where there is not room for my Master as well as myself.

Since Christ suffered while he was in his body, strengthen yourselves with the same way of thinking Christ had. The person who has suffered in the body is finished with sin. Strengthen yourselves so that you will live here on earth doing what God wants, not the evil things people want.

I Peter 4:1-2 NCV

W | W
J | D

What

Would

Jesus

Do?

HE WOULD LISTEN CAREFULLY TO GOD

Jesus wants us to pay close attention to the things we learn from Scripture because this means we are really listening to God.

Whenever a man reads the Word of God, the Holy Spirit is speaking to him.

We must pay more careful attention, therefore, to what we have heard, so that we do not drift away.

Hebrews 2:1

HE WOULD BE PATIENT WITH FRIENDS

Jesus wants us to be patient with our friends. Because we love them, we must always make allowances for any faults they may have.

He who seeks a faultless friend remains friendless.

Be humble and gentle. Be patient with each other, making allowance for each other's faults because of your love.

Ephesians 4:2 TLB

What

Would

Jesus

Do?

W W
J D

HE WOULD ALWAYS HAVE A HUMBLE ATTITUDE

Jesus is King of kings and Lord of lords yet remains humble, riding into Jerusalem on a donkey.

Between the humble and contrite heart and the majesty of heaven there are no barriers; the only password is prayer.

This was done to fulfill the ancient prophecy, "Tell Jerusalem her King is coming to her, riding humbly on a donkey's colt!"

Matthew 21:4-5 TLB

W W
J D

What

Would

Jesus

Do?

HE WOULD BE CONTENT

Jesus wants us to learn to live happily in all circumstances, whether we have very much or very little.

The secret of contentment is the realization that life is a gift, not a right.

Actually, I don't have a sense of needing anything personally. I've learned by now to be quite content whatever my circumstances. I'm just as happy with little as with much, with much as with little. I've found the recipe for being happy whether full or hungry, hands full or hands empty.

Philippians 4:11-12 THE MESSAGE

answers to

What Would Jesus Do?

W W
J D

HE WOULD LET HIS MIND DWELL ON ONLY GOOD THINGS

Jesus wants us to think of only what is true, good, and right.

Great thoughts reduced to practice become great acts.

Brothers and sisters, think about the things that are good and worthy of praise. Think about the things that are true and honorable and right and pure and beautiful and respected.

Philippians 4:8 NCV

W | W
J | D

What
Would
Jesus
Do?

HE WOULD BE DILIGENT IN HIS WORK

Bringing others to Jesus requires time and patience and making the effort to become more and more like Him each day.

Even if you're on the right track, you'll get run over if you just sit there.

For this very reason, make every effort to add to your faith goodness; and to goodness, knowledge; and to knowledge, self-control; and to self-control, perseverance; and to perseverance, godliness; and to godliness, brotherly kindness; and to brotherly kindness, love. For if you possess these qualities in increasing measure, they will keep you from being ineffective and unproductive in your knowledge of our Lord Jesus Christ.

2 Peter 1:5-8

115

W W
J D

What

Would

Jesus

Do?

HE WOULD RELY ON THE POWER OF GOD AS HIS DEFENSE

God has equipped us with special weapons of defense against evil.

It is impossible for that man to despair who remembers that his Helper is Omnipotent.

Finally, be strong in the Lord and in his mighty power. Put on the full armor of God so that you can take your stand against the devil's schemes.

Ephesians 6:10-11

W : W
J : D

What
Would
Jesus
Do?

HE WOULD
CONFIDE IN
OTHERS

Jesus shared with Peter, James, and John how deeply He was troubled and asked them to pray with Him.

Christian friendship is a triple-braided cord.

He took Peter, James and John with him and began to be filled with horror and deepest distress. And he said to them, "My soul is crushed by sorrow to the point of death; stay here and watch with me."

Mark 14:33-34 TLB

What

Would

Jesus

Do?

HE WOULD WANT US TO BE DECISIVE ON IMPORTANT MATTERS

Scripture tells us that when Moses grew up he made a decision to not be tied to sinners and he stood firm on that decision, no matter how difficult it became.

120

Wisdom begins with sacrifice of immediate pleasures for long-range purposes.

He [Moses] regarded disgrace for the sake of Christ as of greater value than the treasures of Egypt, because he was looking ahead to his reward. By faith he left Egypt, not fearing the king's anger; he persevered because he saw him who is invisible.

Hebrews 11:26-27

answers to

What

Would

Jesus

Do?

W	W
J	D

HE WOULD ACCEPT
GOD'S
CORRECTION

Discipline from God may be painful, but afterwards we are better because of it.

Decisions can take you out of God's will but never out of His reach.

Our fathers on earth disciplined us for a short time in the way they thought was best. But God disciplines us to help us, so we can become holy as he is. We do not enjoy being disciplined. It is painful, but later, after we have learned from it, we have peace, because we start living in the right way.

Hebrews 12:10-11 NCV

answers to

What
Would
Jesus
Do?

W W
J D

HE WOULD DIE
FOR YOU!

For God so loved the world (you, me, all our family and friends) He gave His only Son to die for our sins.

There is no father on earth who has as much love in his heart as God has for you. Though you may have wronged, God stands ready and willing to forgive you freely.

"For God so loved the world that he gave his one and only Son, that whoever believes in him shall not perish but have eternal life."

John 3:16

Acknowledgments

Orison Sweet Marden (5), Dwight L. Moody (7,81,125), C.S. Lewis (9), Edwin Markham (11), Ambrose Bierce (13), Albert Schweitzer (15,73), Samuel Johnson (17), Les Brown (19), J.E.E. Dalberg-Acton (21), Judith S. Martin (25), John Dryden (29), George J. Haye (31), Alexander Whyte (33), Alexander Maclaren (37), Charles Malik (39), Hildegard of Bingen (43), George Eliot (45,97), Owen Felltham (47), Oliver Wendell Holmes (53), Daniel Defoe (55), Thomas Fuller (57), Mother Teresa (59), La Rochefoucauld (61), Ann Cummins (67), E.H. Chapin (69), Olin Miller (71), Arnold Glasow (75), Channing (77), Elbert Hubbard (79), Wilson Mizner (83), Philip Gibbs (89), Leonardo da Vinci (91), James Hamilton (93), William James (95), Mark Twain (99), John F. Kennedy (101), John Newton (103), Martin Luther (105), Hosea Ballou (109), William Hazlit (113), Will Rogers (115), Jeremy Taylor (117), Louis Finkelstein (121).

References

About the Author

Beverly Courrege and Boo, her husband, have been involved in the Christian Bookselling Industry for 25 years with Courrege Design, a Christian gift manufacturer. As a designer, she has created hundreds of items for the Christian marketplace and writes as a free-lancer for newspapers, magazines, trade publications and movie reviews. Her closest friends know that writing has always been her lifelong dream.

She recognized a need with the current phenomenon of What Would Jesus Do? - WWJD. The obvious thing to do was to answer some of the questions we all face using scripture, never losing sight of the fact that all life's answers are contained in the Bible. She felt God's pleasure when she completed it and prays the book will have an eternal impact on those who are seeking to "walk with Jesus daily."

To write the author, address your correspondence to:

Beverly Courrege
c/o Courrege Design
9230 Markville
Dallas, Texas 75243